HOW A
DETECTIVE

BY
Mick Loftus
ILLUSTRATED BY
Jeff Burns

MACDONALD

First published 1979

Macdonald Educational Ltd
Holywell House
Worship Street
London EC2A 2EN

ISBN 0 356 06322 4 (paperback)
ISBN 0 356 06362 3 (hardback)

Printed by New Interlitho,
Milan, Italy

About this book

This book has been carefully planned to help you become an expert. Look for the special pages to find the information you need. **RECOGNITION** pages, with a **bright red flash** in the top right-hand corner, contain all the essential information to know and remember. **PROJECT** pages, with a **grey border,** suggest some interesting ideas for things to do and make. At the end of the book there is a useful **REFERENCE** section.

STARTING OFF

Being a detective 4
A detective's office 6
Making a noticeboard 7
Detective equipment 8
Your patch 10
Looking at people 12
Identikits 14
Your own Identikit 15
Photofit pictures 16
Building a Photofit system 17

DETECTIVE SKILLS

Blending into the background 18
Changing your appearance 20
At the scene of the crime 22
Checking for fingerprints 24
Fingerprinting 26
Types of fingerprint 28
Taking fingerprints 30
Whodunnit? 31
A criminal record card 32
A question of evidence 33
On the trail 34
Seeing round corners 36
Tracking exercises 37
The tell-tale tread 38
Footprint impressions 40
Covering your tracks 41
Questioning techniques 42
'Catch the murderer' 43

COMMUNICATIONS AND RECORDS

A detective's notebook 44
Organizing your information 45
A cuttings file 46
Finding out more 47
Keeping in touch 48
The Morse code 50
A Morse buzzer 51
Semaphore 52
Emergency 54
Are you fit? 56

REFERENCE SECTION

Detective books 58
Detective films 59
Detective slang 60
Detective training 62
Index 63

Being a detective

A detective is someone who finds out, or 'detects', what has happened by studying all the available evidence. Being a detective is rather like doing a jig-saw puzzle. Your 'pieces' come in many forms: clues found at the scene, statements from witnesses, snippets of information from different sources. Your job is to collect the pieces and fit them together to make a complete picture.

To be a successful detective, you need qualities of a very special kind. This book will show you how to develop them.

◀ The sinister detective of films and novels. Most detectives are not like this.

▲ The first step in detection work: examining the evidence.

Detective skills

You need patience and an eye for detail. You need a good memory and an inquiring mind. Detective work often calls for long hours with very little sleep. So you need to be healthy and have plenty of enthusiasm to keep you going even when you're tired.

You must also know how to talk to people. Detectives have to get all sorts of people to speak freely and give information, sometimes without them realizing it.

Finally, you need caution, an instinct that warns you of danger. If you go blundering into situations that you don't understand, your career as a sleuth may not last very long.

Leave it to the professionals

Detection is a fascinating hobby. But you should always remember that you are an amateur. Real crooks and villains are professionals. And it takes a professional detective to deal with them.

A detective's office

Your office can be quite small provided it is carefully organized.

Your headquarters

Your office is your base of operations. It is here that you will do most of your thinking about a case. And here you should keep all your notes and files on your investigations.

You may not have a whole room to use as an office, but a corner of your bedroom or a garden shed will do very well. Make a list of all the things you need and collect them gradually. Our picture gives some suggestions. Add a few ideas of your own.

Making a noticeboard

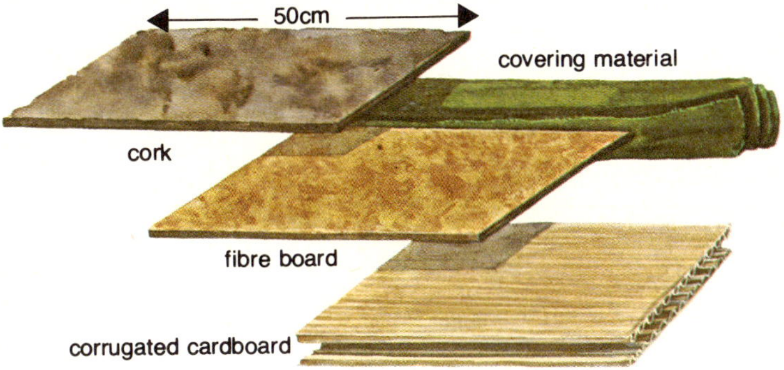

A noticeboard is very useful in detective work. Here's how to make one.

The board
Cut a 50cm square of soft board or sheet cork, about 1cm thick. (Or use several pieces of cardboard glued together.)

Covering it
Cut a 56cm square of fabric. Green baize is ideal, but any other smooth material will do.

Spread the fabric flat. Place the board on top.

There should be an extra 3cm of fabric all round the edge of the board.

Fold the fabric over, one edge at a time. Gum or staple it to the back of the board. Be sure to pull it tight.

Fixing it
Fix the noticeboard to a wall or a door, using a nail or screw at each corner.

Glue edge of fabric to the back of the board.

Detective equipment

A good detective must be ready to act as soon as the need arises. These two pages show some of the equipment you might like to keep handy, so that you're always prepared for an investigation.

You can wear some of the items, or carry them in your pockets. For others, you may need a strong bag or a small case. Needless to say, not all of them are essential.

Wrist watch for checking the time at which things happen.

Torch for seeing in the dark and sending Morse messages.

Compass for checking directions when on a trail.

Map for finding your way to a spot; and back again!

Whistle for calling for help in an emergency.

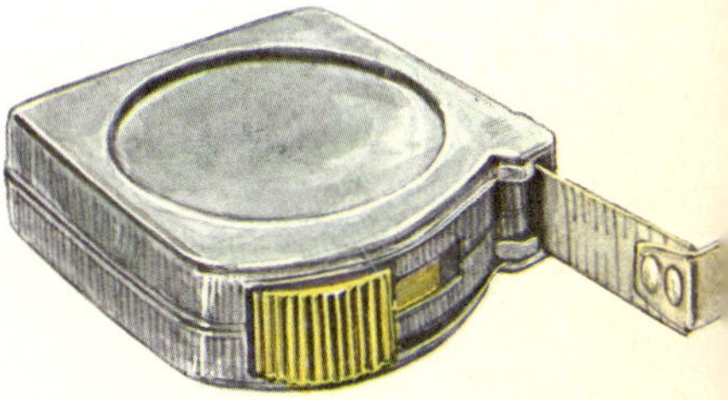

Tape measure for measuring the size of footprints, etc.

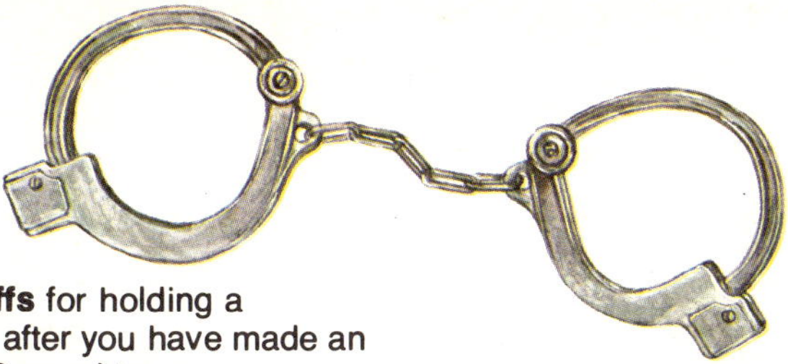

Handcuffs for holding a prisoner after you have made an arrest. (Several types are available from shops.)

Newspaper for pretending to read while on a suspect's trail – to avoid being spotted!

Notebook and pen for jotting down clues, witnesses' statements and so on.

Magnifying glass for examining evidence in detail.

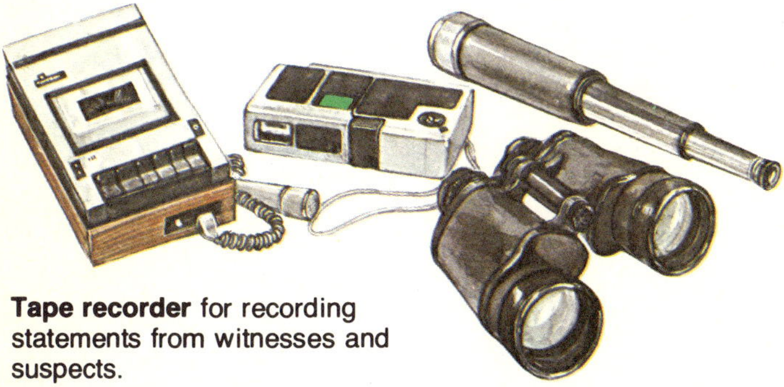

Tape recorder for recording statements from witnesses and suspects.

Camera for photographing suspects and evidence found at the scene of a crime.

Telescope or binoculars for long-distance spying or receiving messages.

Your patch

The area in which a detective works is known as his 'patch' or 'manor'. You should get to know your patch thoroughly. Find out where people live, what they do for a living, and where they go.

The more you know about people's routine activities, the more likely you are to notice when something unusual happens – and be able to help. So keep your eyes open for anything suspicious.

A map

You can keep a large wall map of your area. Use pins to mark the places where you've seen something unusual. You never know when the information may prove useful.

Milk-bottles on the doorstep and newspapers not taken in – maybe there's something wrong. The good detective notices things like this.

Making a wall map

A map is very useful if you want to study your patch.

Enlarging a map
If you only have a small-scale map, you can enlarge it quite easily.

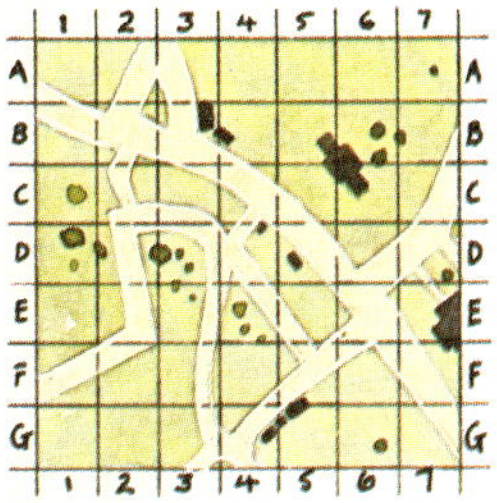

1. Draw 1cm squares over the area you want to cover, as shown above.

2. On a large piece of paper, draw exactly the same number of squares, but make each one of them 3 or 4 times as big (see below).

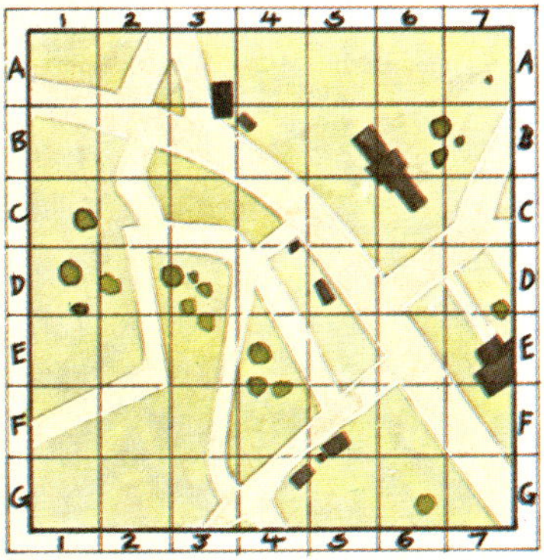

3. Copy the details from the small map, one square at a time, on to the big map. This will give you an accurate enlargement which you can then colour in.

A wall map
You can make a wall map in the same way as your noticeboard (see page 7). Mount the map on a slightly smaller board, fold back the edges and stick or staple them to the board.

You can use flags to pinpoint different areas.

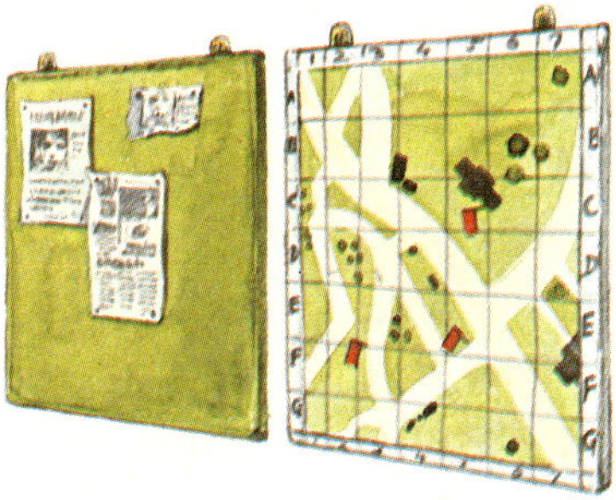

Map Flags

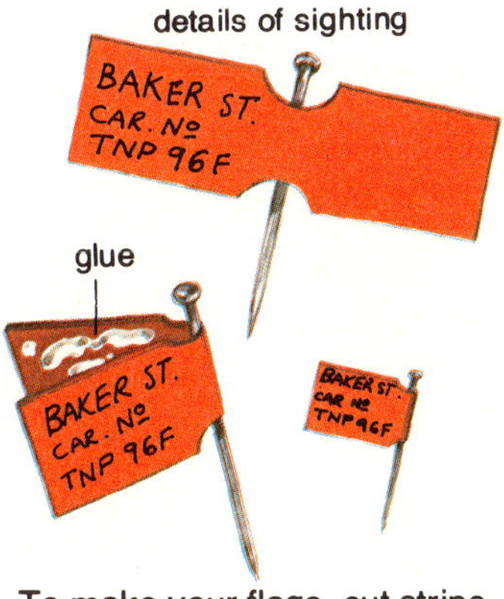

To make your flags, cut strips of paper and glue them on to pins as shown.

Looking at people

▲ These well-known personalities illustrate six basic facial types.

The need for observation

The detective usually only has a few seconds to see what a criminal looks like. So he must make full use of his powers of observation, memory and description. You can develop these powers very quickly with a little practice.

Flip through the pages of a magazine. When you come to a picture of someone, study it carefully. Then close the magazine and try to describe the person you have seen to a friend. Then ask him to find it in the magazine. Keep a score card of results and see how you improve.

The 'checks' system for describing people

It's easy to remember someone with an eye-patch, a limp or a big red nose. But ordinary people are much harder to describe. Here's a simple system of **'CHECKS'** to help you remember what to look for:

- **C** is for colour. What colour are the eyes, the hair, the skin?
- **H** is for hair. Is it long or short? Parted? Is there a beard or moustache?
- **E** is for estimated age, height and weight. Practise guessing these with your friends.
- **C** this time is for clothes. Are they old or new? Neat or messy?
- **K** is for kinks; anything unusual. Bulging eyes, a missing finger, a scar, a tattoo, a ring?
- **S** is for shape. What shape is the face? Round, oval, square or oblong?

By using this system, you should be able to give a good description of anyone you see.

Imagine you had seen this man. Using the 'checks' system, how would you describe him?

Identikits

Building up a likeness

An Identikit is a file containing several hundred drawings of the different parts of the face. There are dozens of different eyes, noses, mouths, chins, hairstyles, beards and moustaches; even hats and spectacles.

By selecting the details of a suspect's appearance, you can build up a good likeness. And you can alter the different parts until it's as accurate as possible.

The Identikit is specially useful for coaxing descriptions out of witnesses. You can go on adjusting the features until they recognize the face they see.

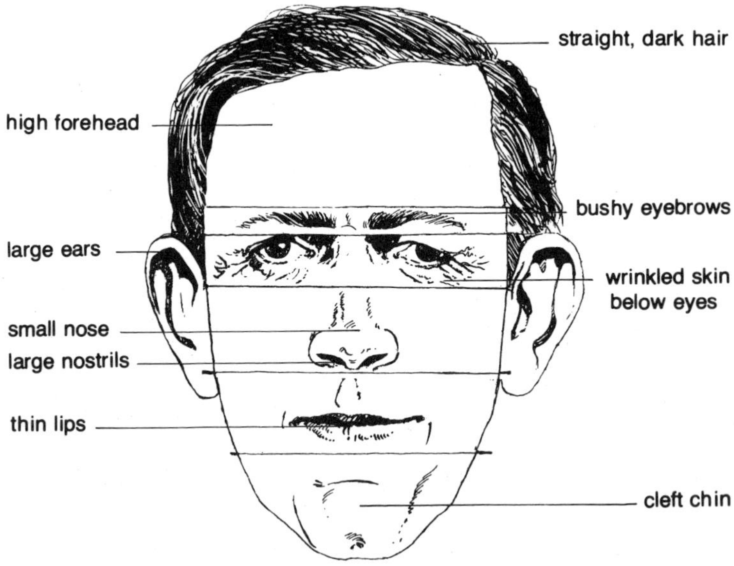

▲ A typical Identikit picture.

Your own Identikit

The frame

Cut 12 sheets of thick paper or card, about 25cm by 20cm. Copy the outlines of the face shapes shown on page 12 onto six of the sheets.

Cut out each shape, leaving the rest of the sheet intact.

Place each cut-out sheet onto a blank sheet. Stick down the edges with sticky tape.

This gives you six basic frames for your Identikit.

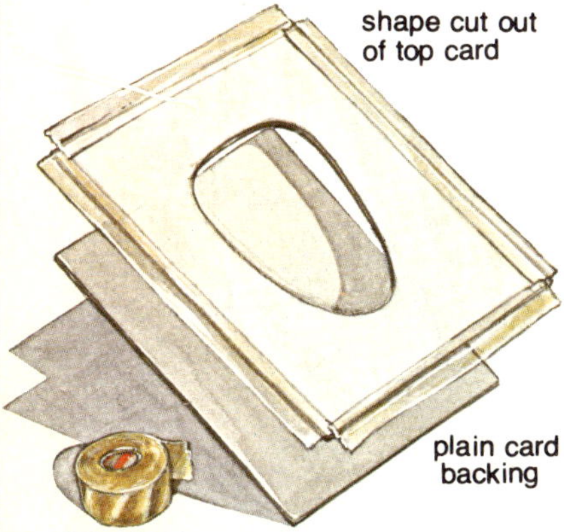

The features

Cut strips of paper about 18cm long. Draw on them different styles of eyes, noses, etc.

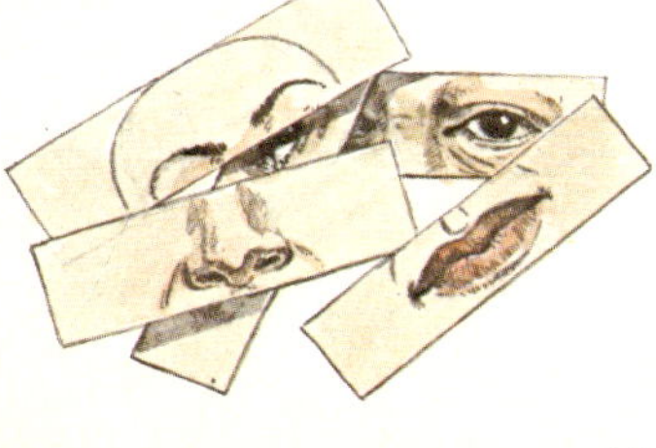

Assembling them

Draw as many different types of each feature as possible. The strips can be shaped and tucked into the frames, then moved around for positioning.

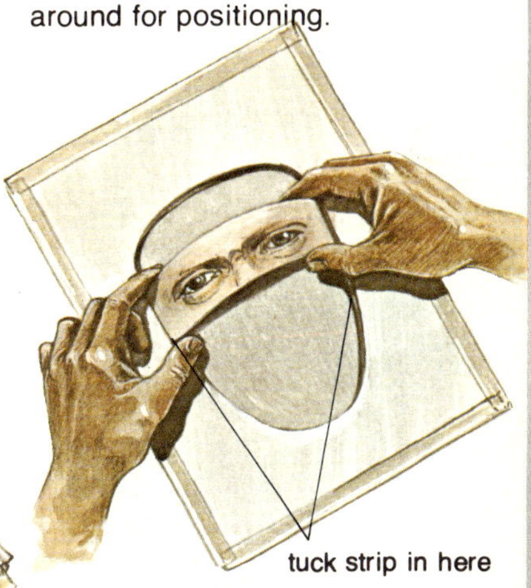

Finishing touches

Finally, draw hairstyles, beards and ears. Cut them out so that they can be placed on the outside of your frames.

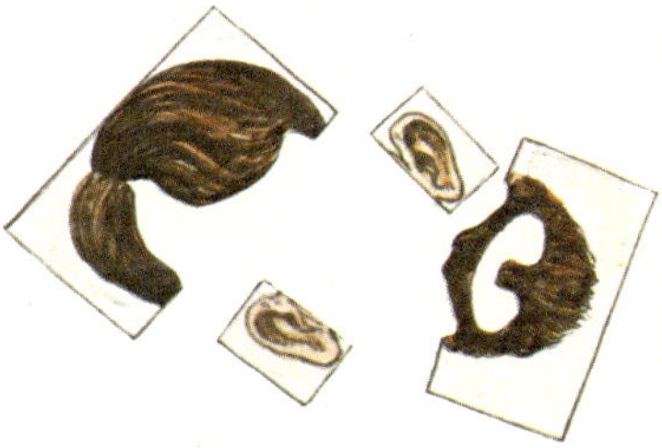

Note: keep all your drawings to the same scale, or the effects will not be convincing.

Photofit pictures

A photographic likeness

The Photofit system is even more realistic than the Identikit system. It is based on photographs rather than drawings. This is the system generally used on today's 'WANTED' posters.

Photofit pictures are made up of details cut from thousands of photographs. They are printed on cellophane so that they can be laid over one another.

Obviously, it would cost a lot of money to build up a real Photofit system. But you can compile your own kit for nothing by cutting up photos taken from newspapers and magazines.

When you have collected a lot of details, try to build up a Photofit of someone you know: a relation or friend. You will find that you need scores of pictures to build up even a reasonable likeness.

A witness helps police to compile a photofit picture.

Building a Photofit system

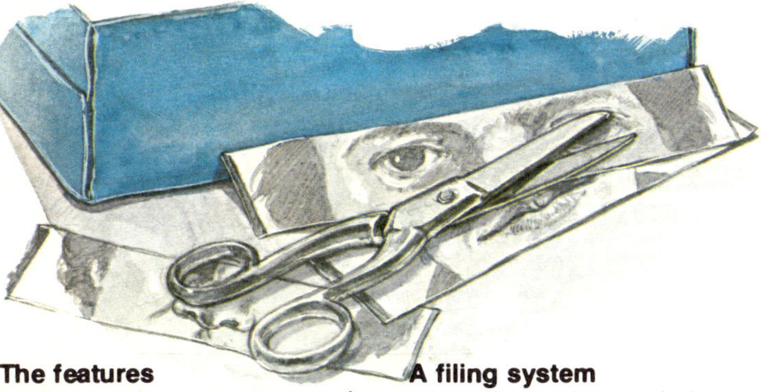

The features

Look through newspapers and magazines for large head shots of people facing the camera. Cut them into strips, so that each feature has a strip of its own. Cut round the outlines of hair, ears and beards.

The frame

Make frames for your Photofit, using the same method as for the Identikit (see page 15).

Fitting it all together

As with the Identikit, slip the eyes, eyebrows, noses, mouths and moustaches *inside* the frame. Let the hair, ears, beards rest on top, at the edges of the face outline.

frames

A filing system

Keep all your bits and pieces of photographs in separate envelopes: one for eyes, one for noses and so on. For greater efficiency, you can put your frames and envelopes into a box file system (see page 45).

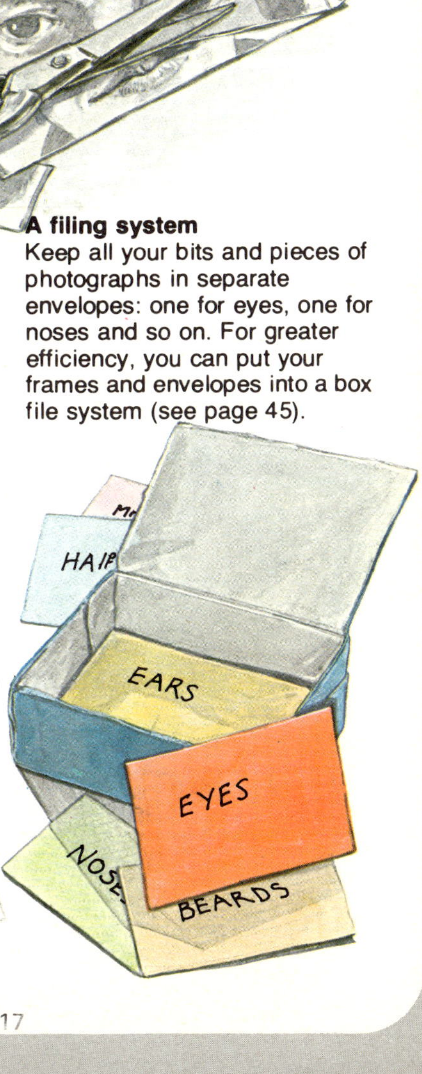

Blending into the background

When following a suspect, the detective must avoid being spotted. He must know how to blend into the background wherever he goes. If a suspect realizes he is being followed, he will be extra careful not to do anything to give himself away.

The right clothes

Don't wear anything too fancy. The more ordinary you look, the less noticeable you will be. Forget the trenchcoats and trilby hats that are popular in thrillers. Any sleuth wearing them would be spotted at once – especially during the summer months.

Make sure that your clothes are comfortable. If you keep fingering an itchy collar or loosening a tight shoelace, you're sure to be noticed.

The wrong clothes!

▲ **Sensible clothes for detective work.**

Carrying equipment

Don't carry anything that will arouse suspicion. Leave your detective's bag or case at the office when you are on the trail. It could give you away, and might be a nuisance if you need to hide in a hurry. Clothes with plenty of pockets are a better idea. They allow you to carry your essential equipment: notebooks, maps and so on.

A folded newspaper or comic is a good idea. You can open it up and pretend to read if you are in danger of being spotted. You can sit on it when the ground is damp and use it to wrap up evidence.

Try to be prepared for the different situations you may find yourself in. If you think a trail will lead you to a beach, take swimming things along, just in case. If it looks like rain, make sure you have a raincoat.

Changing your appearance

Even the best detectives are spotted occasionally. When this happens, you will have to change your appearance.

There are many good disguise outfits that you can buy. Try magic or theatrical shops, or department stores. But remember that grey wigs, beards or false noses may be quite unsuitable for your investigation. In fact, the best ways of becoming a new person are often the simplest. They have the added advantage of being very quick to apply if you are in a hurry. Try out any new disguise in front of the mirror first.

▲ Pad out your **cheeks** with cotton wool.

▲ Try **parting your hair** in a new way.

▲ Put on a **pair of glasses** (or take your glasses off if you normally wear them).

Simple steps to a new appearance

As you can see from these pictures, you can change your appearance very simply. None of the disguises shown here involves wigs or make-up. And none of them takes more than a few seconds to apply.

▲ Put on a **hat** and tie a **scarf** around your neck.

▲ If carrying a **coat**, put it on. If wearing one, take it off.

At the scene of the crime

Let's assume you have arrived on the scene of the burglary shown below. You are looking for clues. You can't afford to ignore any of them, even if they seem unimportant. Remember the jig-saw puzzle: the more pieces you can fit together, the clearer the picture becomes.

▼ The scene of the crime.

▶ **Details that might hold clues. The footprints could tell you how large the burglar is. And the blood on the broken glass could give you his blood type; it also means you must look out for a suspect with a cut hand.**

Method of entry

The door lock is intact. Unless the burglar had a stolen key, he must have come in some other way. How? The broken window gives the answer. The shattered glass has fallen inwards, so it must have been broken from outside. The bloodstains on the glass could give you a clue to the burglar's identity.

Gathering information

Question the owner of the house to find out what is missing. Make a detailed list. Many thieves are caught while trying to sell their stolen goods.

Question the neighbours. Perhaps someone saw the burglar. Can they give you a description? Perhaps they saw a getaway car. Did they jot down the number?

Write down all this information in your notebook. But don't touch anything: you have one more check to make (*see overleaf*).

Checking for fingerprints

All human beings have a pattern of grooves on their fingertips. These leave marks on whatever they touch, although they are not always visible. The marks are known as fingerprints (or 'dabs').

Using scientific methods, it is possible to make copies of fingerprints so they can be kept on file and studied more closely. No two people's fingerprints are exactly alike. So they can be used to identify criminals beyond any doubt.

Where to look for fingerprints

Let's return to the scene of the crime. The room is just as we left it, but now arrows point to where good, clear fingerprints are likely to be found. The best prints are usually left on hard, shiny objects like metal, glass, polished wood and glossy paintwork.

Of course, many criminals wear gloves to avoid leaving fingerprints. But even the cleverest may somethimes forget. Check *all* likely places.

▲ Likely spots for fingerprints.

Points to look out for

Study the room with care. Notice that the chest of drawers has been opened. Did the crook leave his fingerprints on the polished wooden top, or on the drawer handles? These should be checked.

The television set seems to be at a strange angle. Did the thief move it to get at something behind it?

Go around the room and examine it thoroughly. Make sure there is nothing you have overlooked.

Fingerprinting

The detective's 'box of tricks'

When the police arrive at the scene of a crime, one of them will usually produce a 'box of tricks' and start to dust the furniture with a little paint brush. In fact, he is dusting for fingerprints.

You can do the same with the simple kit shown below. The materials are cheap and easy to come by, and they will give very satisfying results.

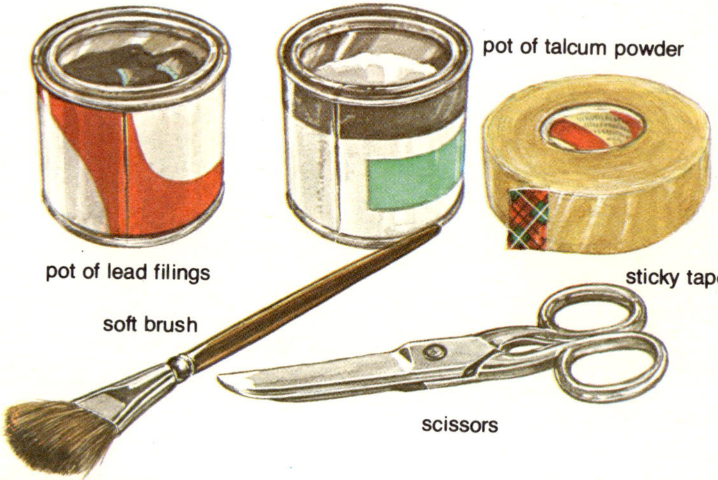

Dusting powders

Strip the wood away from the top 3cm of a black lead pencil. Grind the lead to powder in a pencil sharpener.

Catch the **lead filings** on a piece of paper and pour them into a container (such as an old pill box).

Make a similar container of **talcum powder.** These are your dusting powders.

Use the talcum powder on dark surfaces, and the lead filings on light surfaces, so that the fingerprints stand out against the background.

Other equipment

You will also need a roll of transparent **sticky tape**, a small soft **paintbrush** and a pair of **scissors.**

Lifting a fingerprint

▶ **1.** Choose the area you want to check. Dip your brush into the appropriate pot. Shake off any surplus powder.

Brush the powder *very gently* in and around the fingerprint area. Use as few brush strokes as possible, so as not to damage the print.

◀ **2.** Wipe your brush with a clean, dry cloth or tissue. Now use the brush to dust the area lightly.

Some dust will stick to the greasy fingermark and reveal the print. The rest will be brushed away. You can help it along by blowing – again, very gently.

Having developed the print, you are now ready to 'lift' it.

▲ **3.** Cut a piece of sticky tape and press it down firmly on the print. Take care not to move it around in case you smudge the print. Keep a firm, steady hand.

▲ **4.** Now press the tape harder over the print. Rub it with the blunt end of your pen. You want every grain of powder to stick.

▶ **5.** Peel the tape off carefully. The print will come up with it. Stick the tape onto a piece of paper (white paper for lead prints, dark for talc). You now have a print for your files.

Types of fingerprint

Although no two fingerprints are absolutely identical, fingerprint experts divide fingerprints into four main groups, based on the underlying pattern of the print (see opposite). Using these four basic groups, it is possible to draw up a very accurate description of a fingerprint, which can then be filed for reference.

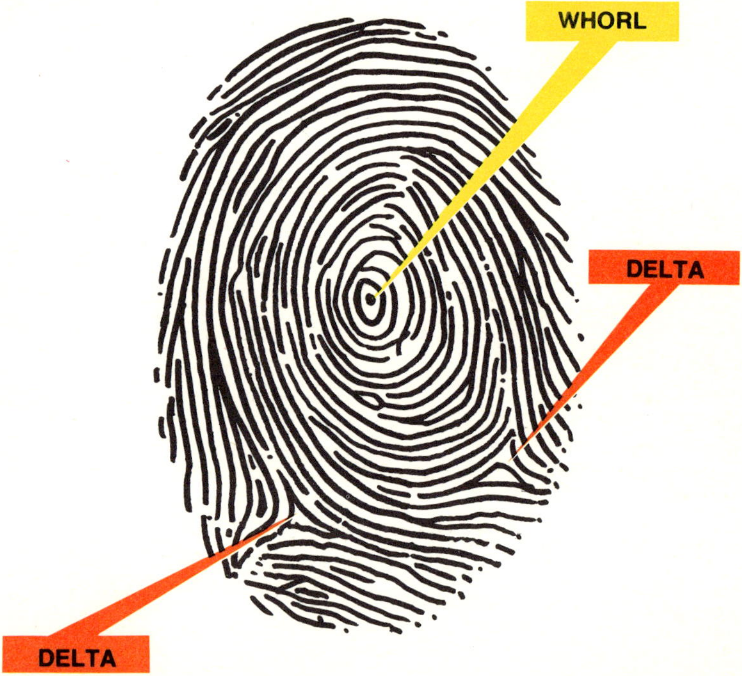

How to examine a fingerprint
When examining a fingerprint, always begin at the centre. Find out which of the four basic types the print belongs to.

Look for any distinctive scars, marks or deltas (where three sets of lines come together).

Working outwards from the centre, count the number of lines between the centre and each identifying mark.

Now check the print against those you have on file.

The arch. Has a clear arch shape at the centre. The surrounding lines curve outwards in the same way.

The whorl. Has a curl or complete circle at the centre. There are always two deltas, one on each side of the whorl.

The loop. The line in the middle of the pattern bends back on itself, creating a narrow loop.

The composite. A mixture of types. The commonest mixture is the 'twinned' or double loop.

This is a complete set of fingerprints taken from one person.

Notice that all the patterns are slightly different from one another.

Taking fingerprints

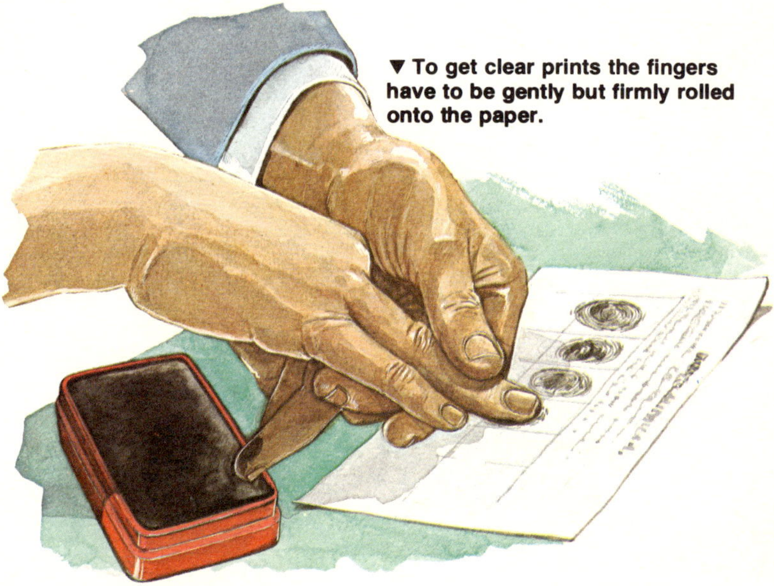

▼ **To get clear prints the fingers have to be gently but firmly rolled onto the paper.**

Detectives need to compare fingerprints found at the scene of a crime with those of their suspects.

Fingerprinting a 'suspect'
You can buy an inking pad from a stationery shop, or make one yourself. Just put an ink-soaked cloth into the lid of a tin or a shallow container. Don't use too much ink or you will get smudgy prints.

One by one, roll your suspect's fingertips onto the inking pad, then onto a piece of paper. Take prints of all five fingers and print them in two rows. You can make proper record cards, marked with squares to separate the prints.

Whodunnit?

Here's a game that will help perfect all your fingerprinting techniques – and amaze your friends!

1. Take the prints of all the people at a party. Put them onto cards and file them in your office.

2. Place a clean glass on the table in front of everybody. Tell them that you are going to leave the room for a minute. While you are gone you want one person only to pick up the glass and put it down again.

3. Go back into the room. Announce that you intend to find out which of your friends has handled the glass.

Pick the glass up very carefully. Touch only the rim and the base. Take the glass into your office.

4. It should not take you long to develop and lift the prints on the glass. Check them against the ones you have on file. Now you can go back to the party and identify the person who picked up the glass.

A criminal record card

A record card is a good way of keeping together all the known facts about a suspect, as well as his fingerprints.

You can make your own record cards of the people you want to keep on file.

Cut several cards, one for each person. The cards should all be the same size.

Divide each card into sections by drawing horizontal lines across it. Fill it in as suggested below.

Criminal Record Card No. 26

NAME: Philip Edwards
AGE: 19
PLACE OF BIRTH: Swansea
OCCUPATION: Clerk

HEIGHT: 1.78m.
WEIGHT: 71kg.
HAIR: brown (long and wavy)
EYES: green
COMPLEXTION: pale
DISTINGUISHING MARKS: scar on chin

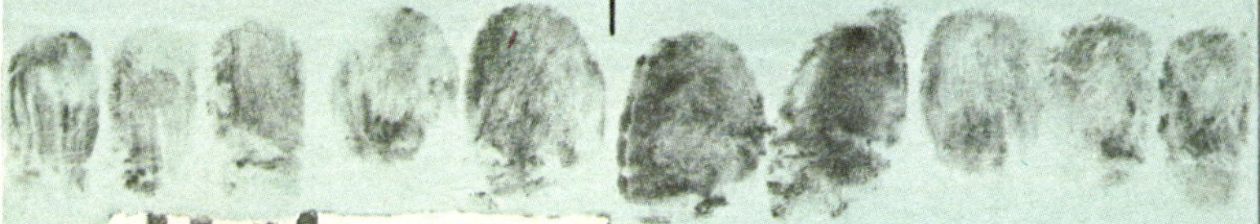

NOTES

Very good at disguises.
Steals from supermarkets and shops.
First arrested 1978.
A slippery customer.

A question of evidence

A broken dog collar by the gate could indicate some sort of struggle.

Without evidence to back your conclusions, you cannot solve a case nor bring a suspect to justice.

If a criminal drops a glove at the scene of the crime, and you can prove it is his, that is evidence. If you can produce an eye-witness who saw the criminal leaving the scene of the crime with his loot, that too is evidence. There are all sorts of evidence.

Handling evidence

All evidence is crucial to your case, so if you find a clue, handle it with care. Pick it up with tweezers or a handkerchief to avoid smudging possible fingerprints. Keep it safe in a plastic bag. Make detailed notes about where and when you found it.

On the trail

Here are a few tips for tracking (or 'tailing') someone:

☐ Vary the distance between you and your suspect. Stay well back on long stretches where you have a clear view ahead. Close the gap when approaching corners, in case the suspect makes a sudden turn and gives you the slip.

☐ Don't always walk on the same side of the street as your suspect. Choose the side with the most cover.

☐ Be ready to duck into a doorway if your suspect looks round. You can pull out a newspaper and pretend to read it, stop to tie a shoelace, or look casually into a shop window. Windows can be useful for watching your suspect's reflection, too.

☐ Don't always use the same trick. If you do, your suspect will come to recognize you.

Office security

While you are out on a suspect's trail, someone may want to get into your office to check up on you. How can you tell if your office has been searched?

Even if your office has no lock, there is a simple way of telling whether anyone has been in during your absence.

Cut a few centimetres of cotton thread, the same colour as your door. When you leave the room, stick one end of the cotton to the door with sticky tape. Stick the other end to the door frame. The cotton should be low down, where it won't be seen.

Wipe the doorknob and the surrounding paintwork with a handkerchief. Then go on your way.

When you come back later, check the cotton. If it has been broken or moved, you will know that someone has been in. Dust the door for fingerprints and you may get evidence against the intruder.

◀ A newspaper provides good cover for a detective on the trail.

▼ An examination of the tyres can reveal where a car has been.

Seeing round corners

A periscope
A periscope is very useful for seeing round corners and over walls.

Materials
To make one, you need: two square handbag mirrors, some plywood or thick card, and glue or thin nails.

Top, base and sides
Cut four pieces of plywood or card to the same width as your mirrors. The pieces can be whatever length you like, as long as they are all the same.

Place the mirrors on the ends of two of the pieces. Draw lines across the end sections. Now remove the mirrors and cut off the two end sections.

Assembling the periscope
Glue or nail the top and base to the back and front as shown. Stick the mirrors in position.

Make sure that the mirrors are facing outwards. And make sure that the distances marked 'x' are all equal.

Now glue or nail on the sides and your periscope is complete.

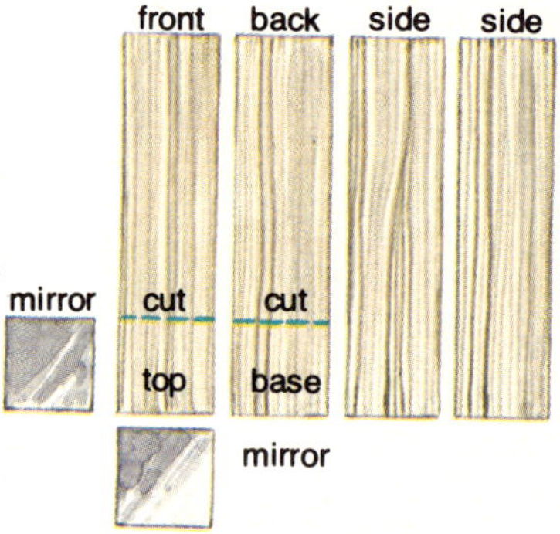

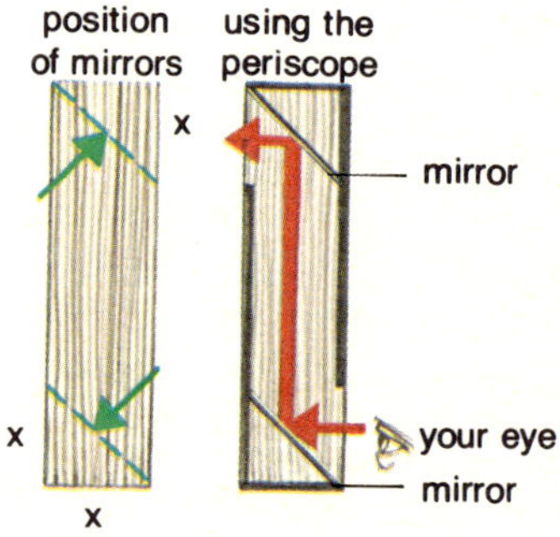

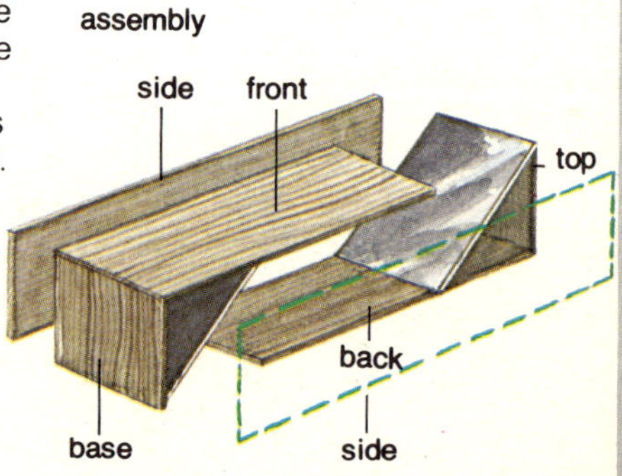

Note: If you use nails rather than glue, be gentle with the hammer. Unless you work carefully you will shatter the mirrors.

Tracking exercises

▲ **Laying a trail with twigs and stones.**

▼ **Directions scratched into the earth.**

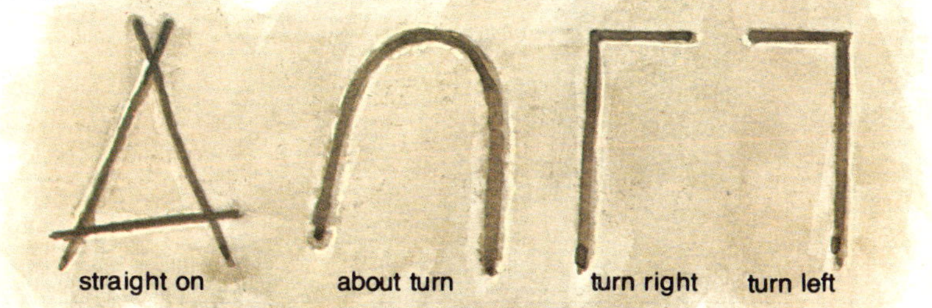

In town and country

Give a friend a headstart and ask him to lay a trail for you. He should leave a clue each time he branches off the main track. Don't use litter. Make arrows on the ground with twigs or stones, scratch clues into the earth with a stick, or invent your own coded clues.

On the beach

Low tide, when the sand is wet, is perfect for tracking footprints. First, examine your friend's feet or shoes, then close your eyes and send him off. Count up to 100. Now start tracking. You may find it quite a challenge to distinguish his footprints from all the others on the beach.

The tell-tale tread

Learning from footprints

Footprints can reveal a lot about the person who made them: what sort of shoes they were wearing, how big or small they are, which direction they were going in, whether they were alone or not. Prints that show a badly worn heel may mean the person is down on his luck. Lopsided prints indicate that something heavy was being carried.

Suppose you saw the footprints shown on the right. What would they tell you about the people who made them?

1. These tracks were made by a man in heavy, studded boots. He was with a woman in dainty high-heeled shoes, but she left him after a few paces.

2. This person wore plimsolls and had a small dog with him. They walked a short distance together. Then the man picked up the dog and ran off.

3. The man who made these tracks had a limp. He could not put his weight on his left heel. The round marks tell us that he also used a walking stick.

Match the prints

Here is a selection of footprints and the shoes that made them. But they are all mixed up.

Can you match the prints and shoes? Turn the page upside down for the answers.

1. Walking boot
2. Child's wellingtons
3. Ladies' high heeled shoes
4. Diver's flipper
5. Running shoes
6. 'Flip-flops'
7. Tramp's shoes
8. Rope-soled espadrilles
9. Plimsolls

Footprint impressions

To keep a detailed record of a footprint, make a plaster impression of it.

Materials
You need water, a bag of plaster of Paris (from modelling shops) and a large bucket or empty paint pot to mix them in. You may also need some salt, sugar and an aerosol spray of paint or hair-lacquer.

Hardening the ground
If the ground is soft, spray the footprint area with the aerosol to harden it.

Shake the can before use, and hold it at least 30cm from the footprint so that the spray falls evenly over the area.

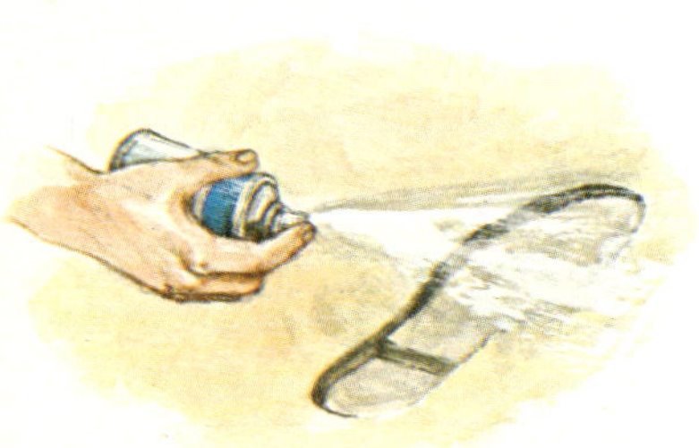

Mixing the plaster
Put about a pint of water into the bucket. Add plaster of Paris gradually, until the mixture is thick and creamy.

The mixture should be stiff, but still liquid enough to pour. If it starts to harden in the bucket, add salt to the mixture.

The right consistency
Two tablespoons of salt should be enough to soften the plaster. To speed up the hardening, add sugar.

Pouring the plaster
Pour the liquid into the footprint very carefully so as not to damage any details. Leave it to harden.

Test it now and then with your finger. When the plaster is firm to the touch it is ready to be lifted.

Lifting it out
When the plaster is dry and hard, ease it up gently. Smooth off the rough edges with sandpaper. You should now have a good impression of the print.

Covering your tracks

While you are trailing a suspect, someone may be tailing you. How can you give your pursuer the slip?

Getting away
In town, walk casually towards a corner. Once round it, sprint to the next corner and get round that too. Your pursuer won't know which way you went. If you are near a friend's house, you can go in and then escape through the back door.

In the country, if the ground is dry, trail a bundle of twigs behind you to rub out your tracks. Shake it from side to side so as not to leave a straight trail.

On wet ground, step only in puddles or on grass whenever possible. You can also lay a false trail by making clear footprints in one direction, then taking your shoes off and escaping in another.

▼ **Walking along a stream is a good way to cover your tracks.**

Questioning techniques

▲ Grilling a suspect.

When questioning suspects, look for a motive (reason) for committing the crime. When questioning a witness, remember that witnesses do not always tell the truth.

Hidden clues

Study faces, hands and mannerisms when people answer your questions. If they blink a lot, or look away when giving certain answers, they may be lying. If they fidget or bite their nails, they may have something to hide. If they bite their lips, they could be worried about saying too much.

Be casual. Make conversation and slip questions in easily. A relaxed witness will tell you more, and a relaxed criminal may make a slip.

'Who's the murderer?'

This party game helps you to develop skills at questioning witnesses and suspects.

1. The party elects you as detective and sends you out of the room. Then someone is chosen to be the murderer.

2. Everyone moves slowly around the room until the murderer chooses his victim and pretends to kill him.

The victim should scream and fall to the ground, as if dead.

3. You are then called back into the room to question everyone except the victim. You can ask as many questions as you like, but the witnesses can only answer 'yes' or 'no'.

4. As you question each witness in turn, watch their faces carefully for clues. Only the murderer is allowed to lie.

5. Eventually, you should be able to make an arrest. If you are right, the victim becomes the detective. If you are wrong, the murderer becomes the detective.

A detective's notebook

A policeman in court reads out a statement from his notebook.

Always carry a notebook. Make an immediate note of every statement you receive and every clue you find. You never know when you may need it.

Also make notes on anything unusual that you come across during an investigation. It could help to clear up some other case.

Your notebook should be small enough to fit in your pocket, but not so tiny that it is difficult to write in. Guard it well. Never leave gaps on the page that could be filled in with forged evidence, in case the book falls into criminal hands. Date every entry, and number each page.

Organizing your information

An efficient filing system is essential in detective work.

A card index file
This is good for keeping notes on people. Names should be filed in alphabetical order.

Cut the top out of a tissue box. Fill it with blank index cards, cut to size or bought from a stationer's.

Make divider cards, clearly marked A, B, C, D and so on.

Now fill in the index cards, one for each person, and insert them in alphabetical order into the box.

A box file
For larger sheets of information – wanted posters, press cuttings, photographs and so on – make folders out of thick card. You should have one for each type of case. Label them clearly and store them in a suitable cardboard box. The box can be painted to make it look official.

For items like criminal record cards or Identikit systems, use box files. Again, any suitable cardboard box will do. Paint it to match the other items in your filing system.

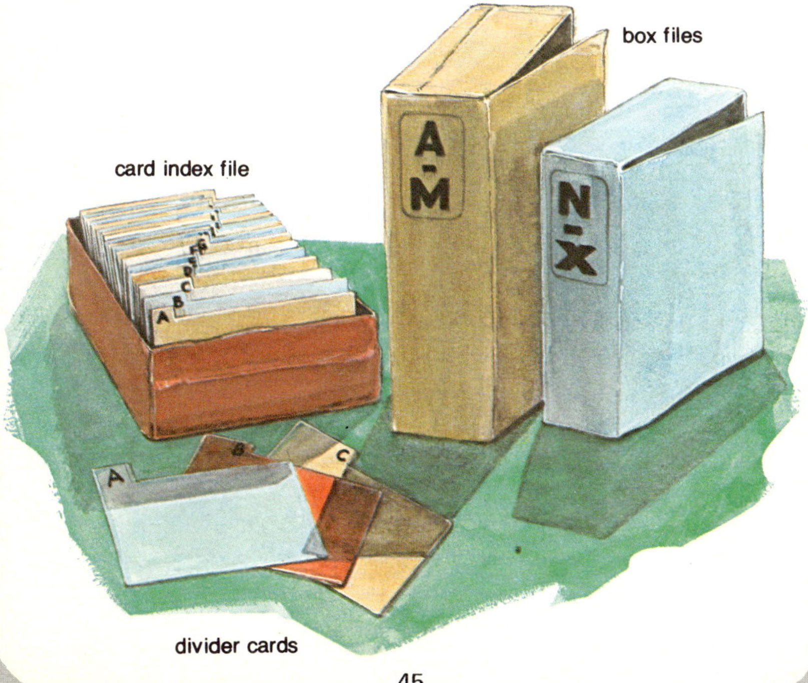

A cuttings file

Collecting cuttings
Newspapers are full of real-life crime cases. You can learn a lot by studying them. Obviously, you can't keep files on all of them. So choose a type of crime that interests you.

You may choose bank robberies or forgery cases. Or you may want to build up a file on cases where science has helped to solve the mystery.

Mounting the cuttings
Cut out the articles that interest you and mount them on pieces of card. You can then store them in a box file (as described on page 45).

Alternatively, you can paste them onto sheets of paper and mount them in a loose-leaf binder. This way they can always be re-arranged and updated when necessary.

Remember to label each cutting with the name of the newspaper and the date.

Finding out more

Very often solving a case means having expert knowledge. The detective on the case may have to do a lot of 'background research'.

In the library
Most towns have libraries and reading rooms. You can find books on all aspects of crime, criminals and criminology. If you ask the staff in the reading room, they will tell you how to get hold of back numbers of newspapers. These can be very helpful on some long-running investigation.

Films
Many films deal in detail with detective work. Some of them are listed on page 59. They will help you pick up handy tips.

Use your local library to do research into a case.

Keeping in touch

If you work with friends as a team, it is essential to keep in touch with one another.

On the telephone
Speak clearly. Spell out any words which might be misunderstood. You can use the international call-up alphabet shown below. For example, to spell out the word ARREST, you say ALPHA – ROMEO – ROMEO – ECHO – SIERRA – TANGO. This is useful for reporting car numbers and spelling out suspects' names.

Messages
If you do not want to be seen meeting, you can use reliable messengers to deliver letters. Another method is to have a secret place to leave messages: behind a loose brick in a wall or under a carpet, for example. These hiding places are known as 'dead letter boxes'.

International call-up alphabet

A	Alpha	**N**	November
B	Bravo	**O**	Oscar
C	Charlie	**P**	Papa
D	Delta	**Q**	Quebec
E	Echo	**R**	Romeo
F	Foxtrot	**S**	Sierra
G	Golf	**T**	Tango
H	Hotel	**U**	Uncle
I	India	**V**	Victor
J	Juliet	**W**	Whisky
K	Kilo	**X**	X-ray
L	Lima	**Y**	Yankee
M	Mike	**Z**	Zulu

A 'dead letter box'.

Codes

You can make a simple code for secret messages. Copy the codemaker and codebreaker strips shown below. Notice that the codemaker *(top)* contains the letters of the alphabet in sequence. The codebreaker *(bottom)* contains the letters all jumbled up.

To encode a message, simply replace each letter of the alphabet with the letter below it on the codebreaker. For example, A becomes F, B becomes C and so on. To decode, just reverse the process.

Can you decode this message: EHWU KR WU HLLWNR?

Making up your own code

Make sure that the squares containing the letters are all the same size.

The letters should all line up when the strips are placed together.

		A	B	C	D	E	F	G	H	I	J	K	L	M	N	O	P	Q		
		F	C	N	T	R	L	A	Q	W	E	M	O	K	U	H	B	S		

The Morse code

Morse code is probably the most famous code in the world. It is named after Samuel Morse, the man who invented it over 150 years ago, and is based on a system of short **dots** and longer **dashes.**

Using the code

You can flash it with a torch at night, or with a mirror on sunny days. You can tap it out on drums, or on water pipes that lead from one room to another. You can use a Morse buzzer (see facing page).

To send a Morse code message by torch, flash once for each dot and dash. Use a very quick flash for a dot and a longer one for a dash.

To tap out the code, leave a short gap after each dot, and a longer gap after each dash.

Learn the Morse alphabet a few letters at a time. Start with **S** and **O**. Then you can always call for help in an emergency, using the famous distress signal, **SOS** (. . . — — — . . .).

The Morse code

•—	A	•———	J	•••	S	•————	1	—••••	6
—•••	B	—•—	K	—	T	••———	2	——•••	7
—•—•	C	•—••	L	••—	U	•••——	3	———••	8
—••	D	——	M	•••—	V	••••—	4	————•	9
•	E	—•	N	•——	W	•••••	5	—————	0
••—•	F	———	O	—••—	X	•— —•—	full stop		
——•	G	•——•	P	—•——	Y	——••——	comma		
••••	H	——•—	Q	——••	Z	••——••	question mark		
••	I	•—•	R						

A Morse buzzer

A Morse code buzzer is a very useful way of sending messages from one room to another.

Materials

You need: two $4\frac{1}{2}$ volt batteries with screw terminals, two door bells or buzzers, two push buttons, and enough twin-core lighting cable to cover *twice* the distance between stations.

Laying the cable

Lay two separate lengths of twin cable between stations A and B. Mark one of them at each end so you know which cable is which. Place a battery, a button, and a bell or buzzer at each station.

Split the ends of both cables by pulling the twin cores apart for about 20cm. Strip each end of its casing for about 1cm. Twist the copper strands of wire to stiffen them.

Connecting the stations

Cut one of the single cables about 15cm from the end nearest the battery. Strip and twist the ends you have just cut. Connect one to each terminal of one of your push buttons. Connect the other push button to one of the other single cables in the same way.

Now connect the remaining eight ends to the batteries and buzzers as shown.

Semaphore

Long-distance signalling

Semaphore is a code for sending messages over long distances. It dates back to the days before the telegraph and telephone were invented. Soldiers, sailors and railwaymen found it particularly useful.

You can signal with flags, like the ones shown below, or simply by using your arms. The great advantage of semaphore is that it's silent, and it is especially useful if you do not have the equipment for signalling in Morse.

The semaphore alphabet is shown on the facing page. Begin by learning a few simple words: 'yes', 'no', 'come', 'go' and so on.

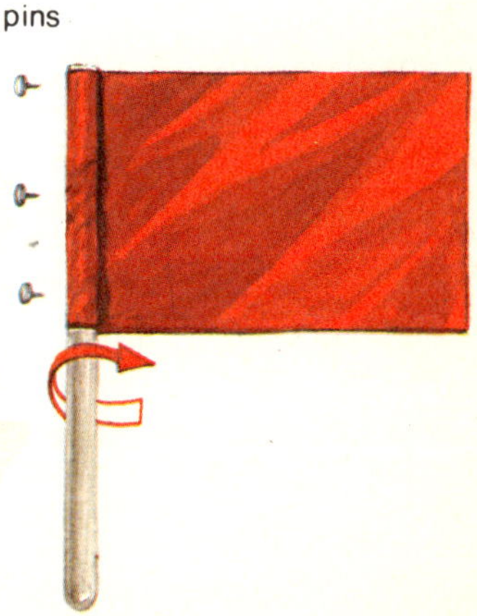

How to make a semaphore flag
Semaphore flags are easy to make. Cut an old broom handle in half for the posts. Also cut two oblongs of different coloured cloth.

Wrap each piece of material around the broom handle, as shown. Pin the material in place, using plenty of drawing pins to keep it secure.

Semaphore signals

Each signal represents one letter of the alphabet. Hold the position for a couple of seconds before moving on to the next.

Using coloured flags helps to make the signals clearer. But you can use just your arms.

Emergency

As an amateur detective, you may be asked to trace someone's lost dog, to find their lost property, or do some task that a friend or relative has set you. But remember: you are *not* trained to tackle professional criminals.

The three golden rules

If you see something really suspicious at any time, remember:

1. Keep out of sight.

2. Pause and think. Is there a reasonable explanation for what is going on?

3. If you suspect danger, *do not* get involved. Tell someone: a parent, a teacher or a policeman. If necessary contact the emergency services.

Calling for help

In a really urgent case, dial 999 for the emergency services: police, fire, ambulance or coastguard.

The operator will reply. Keep calm and speak clearly. Say which service you want and your 'phone number. The operator will put you through.

Give the emergency service the address where help is needed, with any other important information.

The emergency services are trained to deal with danger swiftly and efficiently. You can play your part by telling them clearly what they need to know.

Remember, no professional detective goes looking for danger, and neither should you. You are above all an *investigator*. You are trained to handle information. And if you can pass on urgent information efficiently, who knows? You may save a life one day.

◀ The 'kiss of life'. Mouth-to-mouth resuscitation is a valuable skill. If you get the chance to learn first aid, take it.

▼ Dial 999 in cases of real emergency. Say which service you want, where help is needed, and give your own telephone number.

Are you fit?

Exercise and exercises

A detective must be fit. You don't have to be a fitness fanatic. But you should take sensible exercise every day. This will help to keep your mind alert, as well as keeping your body strong and healthy.

A brisk walk is good for the legs, the lungs and the heart. Take long strides, and swing your arms to get the blood pumping through your veins.

Stretching tones up the muscles. Try stretching your limbs before you get out of bed. Point your toes and push each leg in turn towards the foot of the bed. Then reach towards the ceiling with each arm.

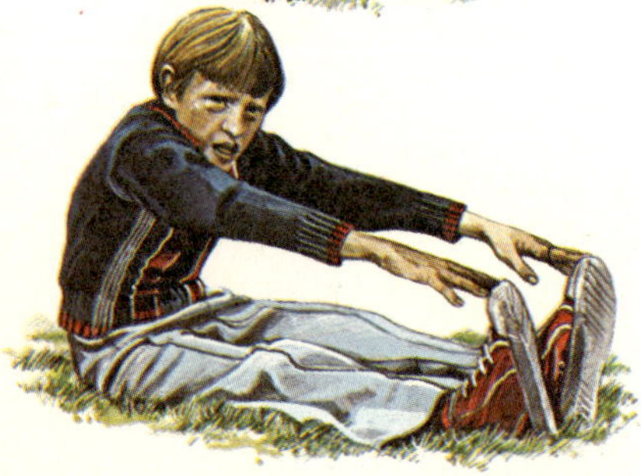

A judo lesson. This form of self defence involves using your opponent's body weight. You can learn to throw people much larger than yourself.

General fitness

When you get up in the morning, go to an open window and take several deep breaths. Hold your breath, then breathe out slowly. This gets your lungs working properly, and makes sure that you have a good supply of oxygen to start the day.

Another important part of fitness is food, which provides the fuel for your body. So eat regular meals. And don't forget, any sport will help to keep you fit.

Self-defence

Most detectives know about self-defence. Professionals have to go through special courses in various techniques: boxing, wrestling, judo. Self-defence is an art which must be taught by experts. Find out about self-defence courses in your area, and choose the one that suits you best.

Reference section

Detective books

Edgar Allan Poe, the American short story writer, is credited with being 'the father of the modern detective story'. In 1841, he wrote a story called *The Murders in the Rue Morgue*, featuring a fictional detective called **C. Auguste Dupin.** In England, Wilkie Collins introduced the detective story to British readers with his novel *The Moonstone*, which appeared in 1868.

Probably the most famous fictional detective of all time is **Sherlock Holmes,** created by Sir Arthur Conan Doyle. With his faithful companion Dr Watson, Holmes wages constant war against his arch-enemy, the villainous Moriarty. Look out for *A Study in Scarlet* (1887); also *The Hound of the Baskervilles* (1902).

Another sleuth who operated at this time was the unlikely character **Father Brown,** the priest-turned-detective in a series of books by G. K. Chesterton.

The 1920s saw the birth of many more detective heroes. Among them were Agatha Christie's **Hercule Poirot,** and Dorothy L. Sayers' **Lord Peter Wimsey.**

In the 1930s came the more violent, 'hard-boiled' heroes: **Sam Spade** in Dashiell Hammett's *The Maltese Falcon;* **Nick and Nora Charles** in Hammett's *The Thin Man;* **Philip Marlowe** in Raymond Chandler's *The Big Sleep*.

Other popular creations include Ross Macdonald's **Lew Archer,** Mickey Spillaine's **Mike Hammer,** Erle Stanley Gardner's **Perry Mason,** Rex Stout's **Nero Wolfe,** Georges Simenon's **Inspector Maigret,** John Dickson Carr's **Dr Gideon Fell,** Leslie Charteris' **Simon Templar** (The Saint) and Anthony Wilson's boy detectives **Norman and Henry Bones.**

Library and bookshop shelves are lined with detective novels, and new ones are appearing all the time. Other writers to look out for include Eric Ambler, Nicholas Blake, Ernest Dudley, Cyril Hare, Edgar Lustgarten, Ngaio Marsh, Josephine Tey and Edgar Wallace.

Detective films

Practically every good detective novel has been made into a film, or several films. In addition there have been many good detective stories written specially for the screen. Some of the older films can be seen on TV from time to time, and others find their way back into the cinemas quite often for 'revival' programmes. So watch out for them. Here's a short list of some of my favourites, but you'll find hundreds more in books like *A Pictorial History of Crime Films* by Ian Cameron (Hamlyn, 1975), *The Detective in Films* by William K Everson (The Citadel Press), and *Film Guide* by Leslie Halliwell (Hart-Davis, McGibbon).

FILM	**STARRING**
Bad Day at Black Rock	*Spencer Tracy*
The Big Sleep	*Humphrey Bogart*
Blue Dahlia	*Alan Ladd*
Detective Story	*Frank Sinatra*
Dirty Harry	*Clint Eastwood*
Gumshoe	*Albert Finney*
The Hound of the Baskervilles	*Peter Cushing*
An Investigation of Murder	*Walter Matthau*
The Lady in the Lake	*Robert Montgomery*
Laura	*Dana Andrews*
Madigan	*Richard Widmark*
The Maltese Falcon	*Humphrey Bogart*
Marlowe	*James Garner*
The Mask of Dimitrios	*Peter Lorre*
Moving Target	*Paul Newman*
The Man With a Cloak	*Joseph Cotten*
Murder By Death	*Peter Falk*
Murder on the Orient Express	*Albert Finney*
Night Moves	*Gene Hackman*
The Private Life of Sherlock Holmes	*Robert Stephens*
Satan Met a Lady	*Bette Davis*
Sherlock Holmes (series, various titles)	*Basil Rathbone*
The Thin Man (series, various titles)	*William Powell*
The Verdict	*Sydney Greenstreet*
Whodunnit?	*Benny Hill*

Detective slang

Detectives often talk in language that's difficult for ordinary people to understand. They use a lot of technical expressions, and adopt the criminals' underworld slang. Here are some of the most common expressions used by detectives.

accessory someone who helps a criminal
alias 'otherwise known as . . .', assumed name
alibi proof of whereabouts at time of crime
APB 'all-points bulletin', a general message
arson deliberately setting on fire

bail money paid to secure release from jail pending trial
bent crooked, illegal, unlawful
bird time spent in prison
black maria police or prison van
blag wages snatch
bracelets handcuffs

canary informer
case to study a building before robbing it
charge the offence a suspect is accused of
clean no weapons on person
clink prison, jail
con man confidence trickster
conspiracy a plot
contempt (of court) disobedience, or interference with justice
cooler prison, police cells
CRO Criminal Records Office
crook criminal
crow thief's look-out man

dabs fingerprints
DC Detective Constable
DI Detective Inspector
DIC drunk-in-charge (of car)
dip pickpocket
DOB date of birth

ETA estimated time of arrival
extortion obtaining money by force

felon criminal
fence receiver of stolen goods
finger to inform on someone
fink informer
frame make an innocent person appear guilty
frisk search person for weapons
fuzz police

gaff house, flat
GBH grievous bodily harm
going straight avoiding crime after prison

grass informer, to inform

heater gun
heist hold-up, robbery
hot stolen

inside in prison

jelly gelignite
jug jail, prison
junk jewellery
junkie drug addict

lead clue, information
legit(imate) legal

manor district
meat wagon police or prison van
MO *modus operandi* (Latin)—the way a criminal works
mug shots police photographs

nab take, arrest
nail apprehend, arrest
nark regular police informant, often paid
nick to make an arrest; police station or prison

old bill police force

PD preventive detention
pen jail (short for penitentiary)
perjury in court, lying while under oath
peterman safe cracker
porridge time in prison
private eye 'private', or civilian, investigator

rabbit talk
rap accusation, charge, blame
rat informer
recognizance in court, payment of money to show good intent
rip-off steal, cheat
rod gun, revolver
rozzer policeman

score proceeds of crime
screw prison warder
shamus detective
shop to report someone to the police
sing to confess, give evidence
snitch to inform
snout informer; tobacco
sparklers diamonds
sparrow-catcher country policeman
spill (the beans) confess, tell the police
stake-out trap set for criminal or gang
stoolie, stool pigeon paid informer
straight legitimate
stretch time in prison
surveillance watch, close
sus, suss to guess the truth (from *suspect*)
Sweeney Flying Squad (rhyming slang, *Sweeney Todd*)

tail to follow closely
time term spent in prison

wheelman driver, especially of getaway car

Detective training

Many private detectives started their careers in the police force, and this is still the best way to get a thorough grounding in all aspects of the fight against crime.

To join a police force, you must meet high standards of health and general fitness. You must also have a 'clean sheet' as far as your character is concerned. Most police forces will consider applications from people aged between 18½ and 30, with a good standard of education. If you don't meet the educational requirements, you may be asked to sit a police examination.

If you leave school at 16 and want to start on your career straightaway, you can apply to go to one of the police **cadet training schools.** These offer two- and three-year courses.

Of course, if you want to stay at school and get some 'A' levels, or even go on to university and get a degree, you will find that these will benefit you when you apply to join the police.

Whichever method you choose, you will have to spend your first two years as a **policeman on the beat,** working in different branches of the police, before your next move can be decided.

If you then want to join the **CID** (the Criminal Investigation Department, the detective branch of the police), you should have shown some aptitude for the work while on probation there. This will be shown on your service record. If so, you may now be given the chance to prove yourself as a **Temporary Detective,** working full-time with a CID branch. If you continue to do well, you will be sent to Detective Training School and, eventually, promoted to Detective Constable.

The work is hard, the hours are long, and very often the results can be disappointing. But if you are truly cut out to be a detective, you won't mind any of these things. You may even enjoy it so much that you'll forget all about becoming a *private* detective and stay on with the police force until it's time to collect your pension!

For information about police and detective work, ask your local careers office, police station, or public library.

Index

The numbers in **bold** refer to illustrations and captions.

age, estimating, 13
ambulance, 55
arch, **29**

bank robbery, 46
beach, 19, 37
beards, 13, **15,** 17, **17,** 20, **20**
blinking, 42
blood, 23, **23**
books, 47, **47,** 58
box file, 45, **45,** 46
boxing, 57
'box of tricks', 26, **26**
burglary, 22, **22,** 23, **23**
buzzers, 51, **51**

cadet training school, 62
camera, **9**
car, getaway, 23
car numbers, 23, 48
card index, 45
caution, 5
CHECKS system, 13
chins, 14, **15**
CID, the, 62
clothes, 13, 18, **18,** 19, **19**
clues, 9, 22, **22,** 23, **23,** 33, **33,** 37, 42, 44
coastguard, 55
codes, 49
colour, noting, 13
compass, **8**
composite, **29**
cover, 34
covering your tracks, 41, **41**
crime, 43, 46, 47
crime, scene of the, 22, **22,** 23, **23,** 24, 25, **25,** 26, 30, 33, 42
criminal record cards, 45
criminals, 5, 24, 25, 33, 42, 44, 47
criminology, 47
cuttings file, 46, **46**

'dabs', 24
danger, 19, 54, 55
'dead letter boxes', 48, **49**
deep breathing, 57
deltas, **28, 29**
description, 12, 13, 14, 23, 28
desk, **22,** 24, **25**
detective's job, 4, 5, **5,** 47, 58, 59, 62
dialling 999, 55, **55**
disguise, 20, **20,** 21, **21**
distress signal, 50
divider cards, 45, **45**
drawings, 14, 16
dusting, 26, 35

emergency, 8, 50, 54, 55
enlarging maps, 11, **11**
equipment, 8, **8,** 9, **9,** 19, 26, **26**
evidence, **5,** 9, 19, 33, **33,** 35, 44
exercise, 56, **56**

faces, **12,** 13, 14, 15, **15,** 16, 17, 42, 43
features, facial, 14, 15, **15**
fidgeting, 42
films, 47, 59
fingerprints, 24, **24,** 25, **25,** 26, **26,** 27, **27,** 28, **28,** 29, **29**
fire service, 55
first aid, **54**
fitness, 56, 62
folders, 45
food, 57
footprints, 8, **22,** 23, **23,** 37, 38, **38,** 39, **39,** 40, **40,** 41
forgery, 46

games, 31, 43
getaway car, 23
glass, window, **22,** 23, **23,**
glasses (spectacles), 14, **21**
gloves, 23, 25, 33
golden rules, 54

hair, hairstyle, 13, 14, 15, **15,** 16, **16,** 17, **17, 21**
handcuffs, **9**
health, 5, 62
height, estimating, 13
hiding places, 48, **49**

identification, 24, 31
Identikits, 14, **14,** 15, **15,** 45
information, 55
international call-up alphabet, 48
intruder, 35
investigation, 44, 47
investigator, 55

judo, 57, **57**

'kiss of life', **54**

lead filings, 26, **26**
library, 47, **47**
life-saving, 55
lifting prints, 27, **27,** 31
lips, biting, 42
locks, **22,** 23, 35
loop, 29, **29**

magazines, 12, 16, 17, **17**
magnifying glass, **9**
make-up, 21
mannerisms, 42
map, **8,** 11, **11,** 19
memory, 5, 12
messages, 48, 49, 50, 51, 52
Morse buzzer, 51, **51**
Morse code, 8, 50
motive, 42
mouths, 14, 15, **15,** 17, **17,** 42

nail-biting, 42
neighbours, 23
newspapers, 9, **9, 10,** 16, 17, **17,** 19, 34, **34,** 46, **46,** 47
noses, 14, 15, **15,** 17, **17,** 20, **20**
notebook, 9, **9,** 19, 23, 37, 44, **44**
notes, 6, 10, 33
noticeboard, 7, **7, 11**

observation, 10, **10,** 12
office, 6, **6,** 19, 31, 35
organization, 6, 45

patch, 10
patience, 5
periscope, 36, **36**
Photofit, 16, **16,** 17, **17**
photographs, 16, 45
police, **16,** 26, 44, **44,** 54, 55, 62
powders, dusting, 26, **26,** 27, **27**
press cuttings, 45
professional criminals, 54

qualities for a detective, 4, 5, 62
questioning, 23, 42, 43

record cards, 30, **30,** 31, 32, **32,** 45
records, 40
reference, 28
research, 47
routine, 10

scars, 13, 28
scene of the crime, 22, **22,** 23, **23,** 24, 25, **25,** 26, 30, 33, 42
science, 46
scientific methods, 24
security, 35
self-defence, 57, **57**
semaphore, 9, 52, **52,** 53, **53**
slang, 60
SOS, 50
statements, 9, 44, **44**
stolen goods, 23
suspect, **23,** 30, 33, 34, 42, 48
suspicion, 19

tailing, tracking, trailing, 18, 19, 34, 37, **37**
tapping out code, 50
teamwork, 48
telephone, 48, 52, 55, **55**
temporary detective, 62
thief, 23, 24
training, 62
trenchcoat, **4,** 18, **18**
trilby, **4,** 18, **18**
twinned loop, **29**
twitch, 42
tyres, **35**

underworld, 60

wall map, 10, **11**
'wanted' posters, 16, 45
weight, estimating, 13
whorl, **29**
wigs, 20, **20**
witnesses, 23, 33, 42, 43
wrestling, 57